CONVINCING THE BODY

By Cheryl Boyce Taylor

Raw Air
Night When Moon Follows

Mango Pretty, Spoken Word CD

CONVINCING THE BODY

Poems by

Cheryl Boyce Taylor

Vintage Entity Press

Printed by Vintage Entity Press
P.O. Box 211
New York, New York 10037-9998

Library of Congress Catalog Card Number
2005931770

ISBN   0-9752987-1-2

Edited by Roger Bonair-Agard
Book design by Sandra Ossé
Author's photo by Artis Q. Wright 2005
Cover design by DL Weber
Cover art by Cheryl Boyce Taylor

To contact author email to:
boycetaylorpoems@aol.com

For my father,
Fitzroy Blackette
And for
Mary Taylor, a great friend

ACKNOWLEDGEMENTS

Acknowledgement is made to the following publications in which some of these poems have appeared.

"In the Name of God," *Long Shot: Beat Bush Issue*
"Americanizing," (formerly known as "Quartet Haiku Arrival")
Bloom
"Summer of Missing Daughters" and "Sunday is for Dreaming Daddy," The *Paterson Literary Review*
"Lipstick," *Callaloo*
"In the Village Underground," "The Pepsi Poem," "Auction," and "Convincing the Body," *Bullets and Butterflies: Queer Spoken Word Poetry*
"Chickens," *Rogues Scholar*

Special thanks to Steven G. Fullwood,
Roger Bonair-Agard, Billy Fogarty,
Patricia Smith, Samiya Bashir, Bob Holman, Cheryl Clarke,
DL Weber, and Eugenia Boyce.
And to Ceni Swinger, for always keeping it real.
Special kudos to Malik, Deisha and David.
To Staceyann Chin, meh yard sister.
And to my band of fierce girlfriends who keep me always strong... Stephanie Cipriani, Christine Boyd Bassette, Angela Holloway, Lisa Bell, Patricia Starek, Deisha Head Taylor, EJ Antonio and RH Douglas.
Thank you Walt for Malik.

"Only the body
is generous, is strong enough
to live past the sugary, hunchbacked claims
of the soul"
-Tess Gallagher

Truth has a way of filling all the uncertain spaces. This is what poetry is.

-CBT, NYC 2005

TABLE OF CONTENTS

CONVINCING THE BODY

POEMS OF GLASS AND BONE
for Audre Lorde

Dear Audre,
what a river of poems you conjured
daily I return to find your graceful hand
laced with weapons
poems of glass and bone

beloved, thanks
you have wired my cells
a garland of white electric notes
knitted to glass and stone
raffia and bone

notes of pine needles
red sand, spanish lace
dried magenta leaves

day after day
I hold your words
careful not to cut myself
paint my face majestic blue
cerulean blue, sea green blue

images fall from my skirt
expose cracked teeth and
brown flaming necks
poems writhe meridians along my kitchen floor

in this small light of evening
metaphors chase dreams
who is that burgundy man
in the wine cellar
that girl in Union Square
ocean folded blue in her breast pocket

can you believe
every night something will disturb sleep
will rouse me
until my pen bleeds
blue unto white parchment

who is this girl
writing notes to the hard earth
when fire enters
leave bone dry.

CONVINCING THE BODY

Study your poems
when you think you're going crazy
lay naked on the earth
cover your shame with praise poems

cover the bright bay windows
curved around a cruel day
make curtains of your poetry

cruise the sky
cruise the sky
find that slight patch of sun

stack poems, two three five
at a time on top each other
add your tears
make a bewitching violet poultice
cover those wounds child

gather acacia leaves
a dash of sea salt
two unruly beams of light

two drops of blood
from one left hand wedding finger
a fountain pen
three diamond nibs
seven wads of paper

keep by your bedside
one flask kerouac
nine sprigs lorde
three june jordan candles
two tablets clifton

ten wads neruda
three large jars perdomo juice
five reams bonair-agard

one skillet two teacups
two steel pans
mountainous garlands of
ai ai ai

your reflection
study your reflection
use as mirror rain water
keep calabash full

trace your mouth
lips deformed and bleeding
praise that mouth and swear
swear to love yourself

study your reflection
watch your eyes
look for crossing buffalo
clear a path ten quick breaths

your heart
strike your heart
strike it child
let it break break

strike it
beat spontaneous poems
from wrist hips
lips fingertips

heart beat violent
irreverent basin blue poems
beat poems from legs
chest eyes breast

now read read
damn! like a poet

FIRST HYACINTH

Oh mother speak
your words written
on this brown paper bag soil

on the lower east side
red painted toes kiss sidewalk
of summer's gown

already the first hyacinths
spring a silver-blue song
a fragrant distraction

in flatbush trini women
shimmer in halters
belly buttons beg questions of war

a flat black pencil
scrawls its name
across one determined eyebrow
secret gospels dance around each lid

TIN PAN HEART

after Trinidad's Carnival Revolution

Lord Kitchener Chalk Dust
Arrow Calypso Rose
bend da song for meh
mash it up   mash it up

chile bring tin pan pot
bamboo bring dholak
bucket kettle an cup
bring de pretty girls

ah do de watusi
twist meh shoulder round
groan bawl roll into de jerk
ai go jump jump wine an bawl

free dem slaves
unscrew shake yu ting chile
move yu hips like a swizzle stick
free dem slaves   free dem slaves

ah go be de jamet
wine an bawl
be de flag oman
wine an bawl

ah go paint dis mas face baaaaaaad
ah red patch over one eye
so ah doh see de lover leavin
cyan see de lover leavin me

ah go wine an wine an wine
shout and bawl
ah go be de nasty dutty mas

ah go wine wine wine
ah go be de jab molassi
if it kill meh dead

go wine an wine an wine
tonight limbo moon
do wha yu want
wid meh shiny tin pan heart

DEY ACCUSE MEH

*"If you do not learn to hate, you will never
be lonely enough to love easily."*
-Audre Lorde

dey accuse meh ah messin up de king's
english wid meh yard talk
bush language back water dialect bad
english smellin rank
smellin like nigga nigga without father
nigga without education poor nigga

de money dat girl mother spend to educate
she
send she quite america for education and
iz so she talking
imagine we shame when we hear de bush
language
she makin dem words long and flat
sharp and mean
slow and vile
up down and wrong wrong wrong
move dem words back back back to find de
black

can you find yu black brown tan white
yellow native black grandmother
can you trace trace trace these words pass
goree island pass moaning ground
hanging trees middle passage tesano
talparo
cocoa sugar cane charleston geechee
port of spain new orleans bahia sunsplash
cropover
can you feel dese words   bacchanal
can you feel de hottin up
gyration is how ai like it
shuffle de feet
go down slow
work de waist   go down slow
shift dat ass
eh heh raise it raise it go down come up
go down come up slooooooooooooow

shake shake stomp stomp wine wine
leggo de slave   leggo de slave leggo de
slave tongue in yu head
paint yu face red black green
yu mouth violet for de blue devil
move yu lips shake dem words girl shake
till yu back slip
water drum make libation
shuck and jive prance and jam call phife
and drum call hip hop call gangsta
ska dub poetry call chutney bangra
reggalipso high life soca call
marley masakela
makeba papa wemba
call sparrow shadow singing francine call
skeeza street walker
bad gal whore
can you read read read between dese lines
lines lines
bend it shake it scream it rape it rape it
rape it
ain't you used to that by now
chile wha yu father name
white
britishgermandutchportugesecyriansoldier
slavemasterlandowner
southerncrackerchristianpreacherredeemer
accuse meh
oh god accuse meh
stalk throw stones break break hollow
from de inside
break me down down down

can you trace these lines
follow these heavy lips
teeth tongue around around these words
back back back to chango oya yemanja
pass bao bao bush creek stream river
water
dirt road sugar bush swamp
pass cutlass pass sweat pass back back
bent back beat back lash whip strap
cuss hate rape missionary offering   back
back bent broken bruised

can you trace these broken words
to the place we first drew breath
can you take these broken words
these words these wounds
this mouth   this body
how long I have waited to talk like this to
talk like this like this

AMERICANIZING

finally
arriving
in america
we grew
new names
dull teeth
tough skin tails
long as benue river

our tears
sea salt
connect
continents
smoke lines
to find our way
home

quiet
quiet now
listen
listen to rain drum
learn to carry
that blue dark heart
close to your mango body
learn to sing
learn to sing girl

learn to sing that bruise

PAN WOMAN

for Lynne Procope

whatever sorrow pan beats down on
will tremble, then up and vanish

oh my steel pan
with your woman's womb scooped out
bruised bougainvillea petals tossed aside

a fine mist of sea enters
a slim silver tune

when the woman shouts, arms upraised
curves her sticks to the heavens

green slats of broken light
cuts through her fingers

when pan screams
her hollowed mouth will call the ancestors

her breast will swell
her womb awake

the house will shake
when pan screams

when pan screams
god's face ascends

from rim of gleaming steel
two blue beams of light

TO HOLD
for Deisha & Malik

A woman lifts her lips
In praise
shouts the sun
thanks the universe
for the hands of her children joined
their eyes a swatch of ivory fabric
torn from full moon

ARRIVAL: POINT JUDITH

after Judith Dupre

Rounding the bend that Friday
Orion a glass tiara hung from sky
a red womb bloomed

moon crossed the road
crossed again
got lost in the thickets

then suddenly the frozen lake
my heart rose a high singing
a breath strangled

with white alabaster skin
moon and her daughters
leapt into our blackened room

the only garments night wore
were black silk gloves
a slight blue slip
covered her female slickness

in the distance
the slender light of Point Judith

GATHER

on the night of the Tsunami

1.
an unexpected kiss simmers
limbs whistle, blare, next morning you leave

questions in the snow
a steaming pot of earl gray tea

love poems on green scented tablet
pink light floods east window

this room moist, lifted
walls licked with your sea

2.
across water
wise women gather

drain shoes dress bone
gather leaves collect stones

this is the moment we burn sage
spill white rum for new ancestors

flatter our children with kisses
deceive god with promises

HEX POEM

for Fallujah

1.
They put a spell on us
Allah, say it's not so

2.
The American soldiers
should not promise the children sweets
it could kill them

3.
His eyes were beguiling blue
such a beautiful boy
says his father

4.
Such a beautiful boy
says his teacher
such eyes

5.
He was my friend
says his sister
they were all my friends
I am only nine

6.
Yesterday, I was happy
only eight what am I supposed to think
about all this
his eyes swim
egg yokes in clear stew

7.
When words are useless
will I be afraid to climb
their rugged backs

8.
Such blue eyes
his long neck a sitar
sitting on his curved shoulders

9.
Trees move together
their heads fuzzy nests
each whistle a wail

10.
They should never promise sweets
those Americans
should never promise

11.
Every family has a corpse to bury
blue tears to decorate their front door
each hollow throat
a red bugle sign

12.
Such a beautiful boy
Allah
say it is not so

PROMISE

Vietnam for David

The American soldiers
should not promise the children sweets
this morning I heard a story

yesterday a girl of war
ran to a soldier for sweets
one arm poised for embrace
his other arm bulged with
lucky charms

she splintered into teeth
arms brains spleen bones
blew a white cracked wind
always in his dreams
in his dreams

IN THE NAME OF GOD

To honor our dead
every September
we light candles sing songs
say prayers shed tears
in the name of God

and all across this land we love
in board rooms
behind electronic wired doors
our father makes new wars
in the name of God

a year of quiet dissolution
the sagging center of us broken
lord America, in my conch shell Trinidad
I drank coconut water, dreamt America
with her streets of spun silk
and red sequoia leaves

America, my new home
I dream magenta Cape Cod mornings
you walk white sheet back roads
confederate hankie flies from car antenna
salsa belch on radio

oh lord, lord your pretentious riches
what this bark of mauby skin knows
stored bitter on these resilient bones

what these eyes have stored
in the rubber of its lids
her flag a fierce lie
hangs in my window

America, my new home
what kind of hunger
eats itself to extinction

George,
what kind of ache
teaches you to run
from your children's hands
small reaching as for bread
smell of war in their hair

you do not know
your own baby's hands
buried in your stern red wrist
eating itself for comfort.

CHARM

Rose early
watched my Brooklyn sky unfold
into a pink bewitching grin
I am forever in awe of her beauty
her enviable charm

THE PEPSI POEM
for Cee

1.
When that girl said
I could give you up
faster than I can my pepsi

I should have answered
with my knife
sliced the diseased tumor
grown disloyal along her stupid mouth

her throat buzzed
a wicked hornet's nest
my poet's brain coma heavy
locked in naïve-blue love sickness

2.
our first storm of spring
exquisite bugle beads of rain
decorate your windshield

there's a silver mist in trees
when night sleeps
outside sky a dusty rose pleading

I miss you, she says

now even these hands have eyes
search her nape of neck
for spider webs

miss you, she says
all that can be broken
Is.

USELESS HANDS

How tormenting a place
the world

when a woman realizes
she has given away

her coral-rich mango breath
for a dull glass eye

her bark shapely legs
for crooked knees

her black beaded dress
for second hand shoes

her blue seminal dance
for the lover no longer beloved

she folds her sandpaper heart
two wings like useless hands

the soul tears
like tissue paper

hear the paper tear
hear the ugly spirits laugh

the hot heart hurls like tin
howls through empty rooms

NOTES TO THE GRACIOUS EARTH

after she left
vinca and begonia
sang rowdy at my window
mountain offered her smoky blue frock

what if she'd stayed
I'd never see fever grass dance
in backyard stream

nor fresh mint
jump the neighbor's fence
hug the feet of red board deck

no country air rushing saintly
through clothes line
arms outstretched awaiting hug

what if she'd stayed

no green pea splitting pod
no sparrow's frolicking beak
no forsythia to press her yellow thighs
through gaping smiles of front porch slats

no racing flame of moon's red mouth
to kiss this gaping earth

FLUTE

Clear rind from eyes
stare boldly into trees
lick stars for no reason

draw the fallen tower
of new york's world trade center around
both eyes
each deserve equal honor

colors must be harsh
salmon red radical green royal blue
recognize your throbbing lips
samba them magic black

never forget
the exploding seam of river
begins in the blue bridge of your palms

a bright red flute runs down your center
rise boldly
blow blow
never look back

NOTES TO THE GRACIOUS EARTH

MEET

poem for Quraysh

us ain't had no hair
by the time we meet

even tho dem locks be gone
dey is still conversin

god's fancy work overflows
ai only smilin

don't remind him notin
lansana and me

pens knitting needles
earth be wool

feels like ah seent dis boy
dis wise red blood

pulled loose from soil
loud smellin marigolds

knows him well
deep in ma goree bones

CHICKENS

father dressed in black
brown paper bag covers his forehead

steals sixteen chickens
from grandmother's wire shed

cries are heard throughout town
when mother wakes and finds them gone

father promises to return them
if mother will marry him

in a rage grandmother kicks
her heavy wooden door shut

earth shakes
in father's face

next day fifteen chickens return
mother cries herself to sleep

SUNDAY IS FOR DREAMING DADDY

Forty eight moons have risen
inside my sacred house
and father it is still you that I love
after all these years

the wound finally closed
and come Sunday daddy
when the thick yellow sun
cracks the half open blinds
I dream of you

in the dream
slim bands of light
pass the chintzy curtains
construct whirling shapes
on the uneven polished floor

your feet a majestic ship
anchor softly near my bed
the raw linen landscape
of your soles
fills the patterns of our life

our love is a tomb between us
I think father   end with daddy
which do you like best

you laugh
ask a question
but when I open my mouth
a stone falls out

I know so little daddy
of this silence
like dark tree trunks
grown stout between us

Sundays when the teakettle hums
the blue flame rocks silly in its frame
I wake to greet your face

high cheek bones
steeled outside a flattish nose
and father it is still you I love
after all these years
your full face folded into smiles.

BLACKEYED SUSAN

yellow daisies
decorate morning table
mother smiles
a river.

WELLFLEET SUNSET

Outside the city
night enters
a lilt pirouette
trees bend
a passing wind
washes inland

ONE YEAR GONE

for Sheila Alson

Snow has filled the
small stamp of a backyard
where in summer you wandered barefoot
against the waist high weeds
said it reminded you of an overgrown lot

these days
I wonder if the squirrels
have already eaten the green tomatoes
Ceni and I planted
or if the peppermints returned this year

this spring lilacs will flame purple
fragrance the yard
as sour grapes fall
tears staining ground

FIRST WINTER IN LIBERTY

Off to New York City
three days gone
trees charcoal brown
now sickly white

they chatter frown
by four each day
sun done gone

with closing dusk
wind thumps thumps
loud as any love-struck heart

three days gone
no buds in sight
what will become of April

blue rush of crocus April
my April
the bright jawbone of God

ANTIQUE BLUE

Even rain weeps tonight
the terra cotta peach roof
antique blue cracked window
gummy green veins of your aloe plant
why
after you
I have half loved
I have run out of names
to call this bulging flame

ICED GINGER

I want again
those hands   curved tropical orchids
eyes   spirited nuggets of maize
breath   river's glitter mouth
breast   loaves of sweet iced ginger
thighs   brown columns to sleep under
no cheekbone more beautiful than hers
when morning opens
her bare chest
a finely sculpted bowl

KITE

My narrow bed calls
more and more
I go to her alone
lay upon her
stark
brittle
brown
straw
there are usually
purple orchids
yellow tail shiraz
la croix in it's trim blue jug
on the white wicker dresser
and a white candle's blue glow
for the small girl
who wants to tie a string
around her pinkie
fly the bright trellised kite of moon

SAY

Here is the letter
I intended to write you

Water: long ago I wanted to say
Wind: your skin, your teeth, your thumb
          haunts me

Breath: and though you can't say it
Moon: the mountains have your eyes

They say you miss me

RAIN GOD

For three weeks it rains
then one morning
we set out butter yellow candles
for Ochun and the rain Gods
a pot of sweet ginger tea for sun

when she is finally here
we are weakened by her beauty
her mouth a sequined sari
hair sweetened with pots of honey

she dons her yellow hat
lord bless the sun
and never let me forget
to pay homage to the rain.

BIRTH

When her belly was rubbed
the waiting child kicked
a vicious circle against my palm

because she was a woman
I let her hands in my hair
let her make a bed
sleep there
and the wise red hungry
breast gorged with flowers
nipples edible grain
her kisses like birth
and I loved
the cheap-ass burly noises
she made breath
a long labored song
hummed through
the rich burgundy interior
where light is made

BIRTHDAY FOR ELIJAH

Like a mirror with two faces
water paints herself here
an amethyst pool breaks empties
I am passing like an heirloom of mystery

I am turning
making that last trip down
stalks of wild flowers filled to the top
red is the color of patience today

native white
the color of her risen womb
I move to the top
saunter down

this morning when the coral tides come
it will not offer milk
just a sharp opening and closing
of sea's crimson mouth

a blue silence ricochets
off the gathering air
night croons with songs
of going home

I fill my basket palm
with things I want to keep
a wink   a whisper
a toothless grin
a spoon of tears

make my way slow
down the long cosmos-pink rope
with only moon for company

speak to me
womb my oldest friend

DIXON AVENUE

An overgrown front yard pine
sails morning light off its loopy frame
the lilac branch laden with fragrance
each bud a sacred rosary

already the stairs open wide
when I arrive
even the stained banisters
have begun to smell like me

olive oil, garlic, ginger
and Trinidad turmeric

too many nights that unsound deck
will hold my shaky secrets
already my heart detests your absence
tattooed to flesh

in a thousand goddamn
red stained wails
tears fold the body

already I am learning the wind
her cavernous wound
against the black open throat
wail of sky

NO DRUMS IN THIS HOUSE

I have tuned my ear
to the melodies of mountain rivers
learning the names of lakes

learning the names of purple and pink
trumpet shaped flowers
creeping past my window

there are no drums in this house
the great dancer's feet are shrapnel
on the butterscotch earth

the one who once loved me
paints her female engine red
for some other beast

for this ritual I offer
a small wooden slingshot
six hunter-green bullets
and a brightly sharpened nail

RULES OF GOODNESS

open heart real slow
smile more, trust less, listen well
run when thunder roars

travel light and leave
anything too heavy, for
good heart to carry.

3

MANGO PRETTY

MANGO PRETTY

she fat
she cyan be pretty
if yu fat fat fat no way in hell yu could be
pretty

all she do is eat eat eat
how she could be pretty
no modern man eh go want she
only food food food
yu cyan be pretty   pretty fat

look at she
big face
big teeth
big mouth
big tits
big tummy   no
nonono   no way
no way
she cyan be pretty
who go want she

de white man say say say
elle in style essence   say say say
ebony   say say say   she ugly
new york times   say say say too fat fat fat
to be pretty

ah mean...long bouncy hair smooth chin
light light light unblemished skin
uh huh pretty pouty lips
straight nose tiny ass barbie feet
now that is pretty
white white white skinny skinny
white white white
wannabee wannabeee white
white blackwhittteeee girls
black black nappy blackwhite girls
they pretty

ah mean
yu could eat eat eat
bu yu mus puke puke puke
then then then yu could be pretty pretty
pretty
yes pretty so slim and trim
and pretty

long hair straight nose pouty lips
slight nigga booty
blue eyes long long braids extensions
blond blond blond braids gold teeth
puke puke puke pearly white skin puke

douche bag
x-lax
chiney diet tea   skinny
losin teeth   size one size two bad breath
thin thin thin   is in
pretty pretty pretty
not fat like she   size one size two
skinny skinny fashion skinny

eat eat eat   now now now   puke puke
puke
now yu pretty   yes yu pretty now yu
pretty   yes yu pretty
pretty pretty   pretty barbie

not fat like she
wid she food food food
so ugly
rice and peas
curry chicken
brown stew
fat fat fat chicken gravy

fry bake   saltfish
cocoa bread
crab and dumplin
white bread
callaloo pig feet
mutton chops
fat fat fat chicken gravy

she fat fat fat
and *knows she's pretty*
yes pretty   *mango pretty*
black and sexy just ah...slight slight slight
bit nasty
big booty soft tummy for her baby
or her maybe
well round and full

Island beauty
and dey greedy
cause dey grab she
just to taste she
and she big big big
sweet big big big
strong unruly fem butchy
big mouth big lips big arms big hips big
kiss

and she are famous
love she food love she poetry love she
mudder
big mouth
big ass
big brain
love she son love she daughter
love she friends
love she trees
long walks quiet streets

and she big
damn big big money
big words
big heart
big love
big feet

and she big
yes big
damn big
da doh make she ugly

he say she fat an black and ugly yu know
just because just because   just because
she ain't skinny
why she cyan be pretty
who yu to say she soooooooo ugly
to fat fat fat to be pretty

but she pretty
pretty pretty
pretty happy
big brain big plans   big goals
big mouth   big tongue big kiss

an de love she big heart big hands big soul
so what she big
yes big damn big
big big

so what she big
big big
fine big

she cyan be pretty

BLACK

1.
she be a black woman
born between a town's whisper
and a slither moon

she be Ibeji woman
born in hard crop guava season
between calabash and casava
she be the dust of Arima mountains

2.
this skin is a black language
cadent and regal
brown of the cola nuts
from which all nations rise

3.
I carry the wail of tribes in my skin
my mouth jeweled with Africa
would lay down my life for
this black skin

this skin is a temple
where the gods meet
to shout perfection

SHOUT

ON GOREE ISLAND

there are bones
growing at the lap of sea
small off-white like human teeth

have not eaten in days
cannot tell what grandfather's tree is saying
it screams
the rank smell of blood
when they come for him

wind turns down her bragging mouth
waves eat hungry the land
see grandmother's hands
poised for begging

return our good land wracked with bones
three letters and two poems to her daughter
heart a carved brown bowl
the pink billowing
of her growing belly

to satisfaction hate has filled me
all around there are bones
small off-white
at the lap of sea

AUCTION

after the slave house in Goree Island

Mute in the market place
skin fades into the dirty black walls

they shout scream
pitch prices

measure my angular head
stained-white milk teeth

measure bust line
nipples weight height shoe size

over my head the gifts of Christ
cross bible cock whip white man chains

laughter of the slave gods
this terrible sin unpaid

remove ankle weights neck chains
wash, scrub down

I am a wild horse
key turns in massive silver lock

I sneak a glance
my shiny obsidian face.

SMOKE

hot fear
falls around us
thick black smoke

hot fear falls
around us
smoke black thick

LIPSTICK

In Dakar I watch a girl
of eleven or so
sift pebbles from rice
her pile of pebbles grow
larger than the rice
piled at her feet

she peels oranges
hangs the peel to dry on vines
to use for stomach ache

give me lipstick
lipstick for Mama
she pleads
in the way she would ask for
more rice

lipstick please
her eyelids a small jeweled necklace
glows in noonday light

what's it like
to give your daughter
to the world
her face ripped in two

YAPPE VILLAGE

Violet berries paint her lips
bones delicate plumes in her hair

SUMMER OF MISSING DAUGHTERS

summer 2003

Come child let us hold each other
before the leaves turn brown
in this short lived wench of summer

some stranger has occupied this bed
sixteen years
eyes half closed
mouth bulging with blue Geraniums

summer heat thick as winter porridge
slow upon your sliver tongue

loneliness flares like lightening
to singe our hearts
and burn the new green tint
off white Iris and Sweet William leaves

our sixteenth year of questions
what remains

in the flattened blue landscape of evening
tenderness like curtains hang between us

what remains
my arms
daughter
won't you take them

FOR MARY TAYLOR

Under black taverns of skeletal trees
hung morning
fog   weaves pretty straw
                           hang poems
round moon neck
dawn calls   a red day loose
                           a wisp of fire
calls her arms home.

SHOUT

1.
Mother's
laugh
moan
rattle
clatter cry
shrill bells
night
air high
high
church steeple

alone
at his birth
her hands
red rock
break child
rear city
blue
from her earth

2.
If water could talk
It would moan
break
red rock
bahia
nile
atlantic
benue
up lopinot
door of traveling
mississippi
cape coast
maracas bay
elmina castle
holla
holla
him

birth
break him
rear city
blue echo
dawn

AFRICA

she cried
for years
hollowed out skulls
bones
mountains

tree bark
root sap
middle passage
sea's gloomy mouth

at the center of moon a womb
holding all the babies
she had ever left

her wound lying open
for the next blue breeze
to find her

lips dark as Volta River
no mother has cried so
for her children

LOAVES OF BRIE

for Jayne

had we raked leaves
we'd notice trees gathering empty
house ill-shaped with winter

on the kitchen table
two sleek loaves of brie

5

MILK BREATH

MILK BREATH

for my twin brother

Decades pass
then one day his face calls
from a peacock-colored frame
of a Ghanaian snap shot
right there on a dirty street corner
in Accra you remember the boy

you remember his milk breath
his hunger
his bony knees
pressed into your ribs

you remember how his sweet body
pushed against yours
until there was no air
only pulled skin impaled on a gnarled wrist

you remember how his little fist
beat against the door
beat against the door of your mother's womb
to save you both

and later
you sure hope
he took you in
hair, bone, spit, spine, spleen, split nails
knees, knuckles, ovaries, areolas

you take him deep
in the bough of your shoulder blades
deep in the pale straw of your palm prints
you fill up with the brown-nutmeg
curve of his newly formed elbow
his hollow prickly scalp soft along the center

you remember his love songs
sung in C minor
how he made you laugh
when he twitched his nose
into a tree trunk

pulled his eyes into long zippered slits
with teeth, bone and raised flesh
how he strummed your face like a guitar
until sleep settled in
then magga, like wings his legs
shelter, straddle, rock

later you remember
the slack blue flesh of his neck
the line-laced blue of his hands
damp and beautiful
like the underside of leaves

and you remember
blue this is why *blue*
yes, *blue* in any shade
became your favorite color
Iris and morning-glories
your favorite flowers

you remember the drunken cave
of his chest
the murmur-mad whistling
of his lungs

the warnings of how he'd take
you too if you didn't run
you remember his half-smile
the gray cloud-laced blink of his eyes

and the leaving
the letting go was simple
quick   still
his ear fanned graceful along
its curled stem crimson-pink
flushed with living

and in that moment you knew
you could bend like him
break like never

but the sea
the black earth sea soil
rose quiet to greet him
his eyes emptying into the
ocean's steam

and you furious, broken
retched mouth howling
pulsed with pebbles, seed, seaweed
fissures of moss stained bones

wrecked with the stench of death
ache a white vat on your skin
tumble, widen in that vast
mountain of wind

MAKING A BOY

My belly swells as Mausica river
I wanted the cowry shells
to tell me you were a girl

this night I pray
river stays calm within its shoulders
not like that time
in a mad furor its wind like wings
plucked my Easter hat from my head
and gave it to river

I never got it back
whomever you are child
tonight I swear to let you keep your voice

a sweet clear ocean
pulls me to her bridal bed
the seed he planted
grows a love tree in my gut

breasts heavy sore
your father lathers them
with cocoa butter
he shakes out the doormat
lays blankets in the sun

fear welling up in his eyes
when I say *it hurts to speak*

and from my thighs
fell two blue storms
one to clap and whirl
spin spill words
one to stand mediator before Oya

we buried your brother
later that day
earth was black
save for the moon

for five days straight
rain cursed the dirt
as did I
salt covered land
the bed where I labored

and from my tears
came your eyes
the loveliest shade of brown and red
tinged as Arima dust

I embrace my fortune
my son
your mouth an overflowing gourd
may your words never give warning
never give warning
never give warning of their coming.

SPICE

for Malik

after her phone call from Texas
you pelt frozen peas
collards, pasta in the pot
hot water dull, smoky
makes a soft, pink spot
in the frozen chicken

a track star
you chase around the kitchen
from cabinet to cupboard
sink to fridge, dust bin to
utensil drawer

garlic, salt, lemon pepper
piri piri, jerk, organic ginger
flavors Georgia night

and I wonder
what I've taught you city boy
man lover almost husband
is it enough for these prudent days

how I hardly recognize that magic boy
sprung from twins and sparkly dust
long incubator hospital stays
blood snuffed from tiny heels

this morning you screamed
when I opened your bathroom door
all grown up
new tender frame dark caramel eyes

eyes that once cajoled
made me change my mind
a *sorry mommy grin*

putty in those hands of play
punishment changed to kiss
okay go, but come early

now so much like your father's
I watch your hands
remove from oven
chicken steams nutmeg brown

fresh from Texas
that sweet woman at your side
a smile breaks
from the wrinkle of your eyes
spice fills the room
you gesture sit.

NO MUNDANE OPTIONS

CLOVER AT MY FEET

for Patty at Dodge Farm

In search of four leaves
my friend Patty
finds a five leaf clover
seeks a place to store it
keep its life

she tucks it in her four ring silver
on middle left hand finger
it would look sultry in her hair
baroque between her teeth

she stops for coffee
EJ and I move on
when she returns
her good luck is gone

I ask where her charm is
lost, she says
but never is the magic
with which she plucked it

her face a magnificent lake
her sinuous laugh
riding its chopped waters

IN THE VILLAGE UNDERGROUND

Underground in the village
of this veiled city
where the subway does its iron dance

air removes itself
from bodies grown thick
and sweet with sweat
eyes round and hard
dull as rusted metal

underground there is a fear inside me
as heavy as a hand
beneath our city
the music of river runs in stages

collides with nightmares
and all our dreams run together
the dull hooves of silence closing in

it is raining in my village underground
family woes run together
slick as sewer rats
not one goddamn thing
matches this wail

one begs money for homeless
offers food
she looks hungrier than most
one begs money for his break dance
body contorts into seizures

newly out of hospital
another begs money for
medications

with bells and maracas
four men beat drums
spout poetry evoke Yoruba

their women drill white
wail in spanglish
call Ogun, Ogun father of metal
road master of the underground

and all her saints
all her gods fall to the floor
I know her eyes
I know that call

there is a fear inside me
heavy as a hand
my second skin
a flaming city

CONVERSATION ON THE IRT

I be on dey job
hell yeah
dey be searching for me
shit,
ain't that why de call it job search

GEOGRAPHY OF A FACE

Mouth a large crack in the sidewalk
filled with rain water
teeth long black uneven railroad tracks
eyes a fetish corpse
his nose to my amazement
a bruised bartlett pear
he too turns out to be
a member of the rose family
smile a styrofoam plate

ON BOURBON STREET

1.
On Bourbon Street
legs of a sequined mannequin
slither out the window

in her teeth
my used to be lover
catches colored beads
thrown from a stagnant balcony
with promise to reveal a below the waist
gift

I offer sparkle painted toes
in daring blaze of sleazy red

some say
this town's a dying whore
with her orange eyes gorged out

a wreath of broken hearts
frame every paint chipped door
each curtain a monument
streaked with sin

each curdled laughter
clings to some lost clapboard dream
whores that laugh and sell
laugh and sell
a full Jazz broken

2.
across the parched terrain
milk is scarce
gasoline's the price of whole wheat bread
over there they burn human bones
to keep warm

and is this beer watered down
said the new bride
she passes the bottle   holy
we take it
a laying on of hands

rings of cigarette smoke
climb the sleeping night
outside the world seesaws
unbalanced in its un-doings

the good earth loosens her bra
brown tits unfurl
hacks bibles bile blood
teeth   stray bullets stone
felled oaks

in the morning
a bleached ghost town
looms in yellowing day

REACHIN TRINIDAD

yu know when yuh reach home
dey ha to dig up in yuh barrel
he ask meh who all da american food for
ah say
take some
yeah man
take a lil something for de chiren

yuh know how chiren ha bad habit
eh hungry but go eat anyway
whatever yu want take

after dat
ah pass through
voosh voosh

LAST VISIT HOME

letter to Dr. Eric Williams

Three stink frogs
and a family of black goats
liming under a tree
smiling at we
more peaceful than these new island folks

by eleven o'clock in the morning
food finish
roti done
dey rather stupes and gi yuh bad eye
instead ah start a new pot

and I wonder Dr. Eric
maybe yuh feed dese Trinis
too much ah themselves
now dey blue black wid nasty
head hollow like conch shell

NO MUNDANE OPTIONS
after Jean-Michel Basquiat

A small child falls crown first
first blue crush of skin
weigh hard between his legs
legs a crumbled fork

green easter suit
suits his fancy
fancy his black halo
halo grows from strained mouth

that turkey with the gun
delivers smooth control
climbs the rugged stairway to the brain
brain whole voltage music

in the thin air
a brown sombrero moves
moves brilliant
brilliant drum of chin rises

AFLAME

1.
In the upper room
at the twenty first street bookstore
I sing to this pen
and ten thousand books

blue ink makes a lacy henna
on right hand fingers
these stains and over priced coffee
in sizes tall, grande, venti
promise a privileged life of poetry

at closing I walk the eight blocks home
mistake lamp posts for poets
plastic trash bags for shitting dogs
the hunter-green edge of evening
for company

my teeth are a clanging train
on this first January day of brutal winter
the dark bat of your sweet hand
missing from my waist

2.
once at Christmas
I searched the city
to find you white amaryllis
honey falling from my tongue
when everywhere I spoke your name

this year I send you
a box of tissues
spring water
your favorite cigarettes

say what you got to say woman
speak my deception
brown as phlegm
carved in your acrid throat

go ahead
betray me
now
quick

then let me walk back
to my life
burned
beautiful
aflame

BLACKOUT

for Ceni

That last night in stone haven bay
the world went black
Ceni girl, only light available
was the glow from your *newports*

we opened our veranda door
to the light of heaven
snuffed our persistent grins

the unfinished red roar of night
burning a low growl
deep inside

ELECTRIC BED

Mostly now you are gone
In the hours while earth sleeps
I hold still my screaming cells
miss the L-shaped scar on your neck

repeatedly at night
I listen for the irregular tip
tip tap of your too short
beautiful right foot on the stair
your voice drawing breath
from Forsythia's yellow throat

how that generous mouth
held my whole body in place
limbs blazed like shiny quartz
in our electric bed

TOBAGO

Up a trail of warm rocks
and bamboo shoots to the river
balisier like mad red dogs
open their slight yellow palms

when I open your palm
dark heirloom lines
map secret temples

sun a tilted teacup
spills her orange taffeta grin
upon the mocha earth

I could follow the siren lines
of your smoky spine anywhere lover
let me plant guavas in your hair
eat curried rice off your tummy

bind my arms
mount me slow
convince this body

vulgar rough defiant
if I cry I'll blame the poem
taking root inside me

night extends her bluish arms
blanket curved shoulders of trees
what mad delight washed us up
on this delicate bank
your thighs so Friday night

a thin glitter line outlines our frame
darling, have we scorched the river bank?

KNOWLEDGE OF SEA

Your curled torso
a perfect yellow rune beneath hers

her backbone sings
sea enters

now fasten your ear
to the brown earth
of her falling voice

ABOUT THE AUTHOR

Born in Trinidad and raised in New York City, Cheryl Boyce Taylor is a poet and teaching artist. She is the author of two collections of poetry, *Raw Air* and *Night When Moon Follows,* and the spoken word CD, *Mango Pretty.* A recipient of the Partners in Writing Grant, she served as Poet-in-Residence at the Caribbean Literary and Cultural Center in Brooklyn, New York. As a teaching artist, she has led writing residencies for Poets House, Poets & Writers, The New York Public Library, Urban Word, and at her own retreat, Calypso Muse.

Boyce Taylor's texts, "Water" and "Redemption", have been commissioned for Ronald K. Brown/Evidence Dance Company. Her poems have been anthologized in various publications including, *Callaloo, Bloom, Long Shot: Beat Bush Issue, The Paterson Literary Review, Def Poetry Jam:Bum Rush The Page* and *Bullets & Butterflies Queer Spoken Word Poetry.* Boyce Taylor holds Master's degrees in Education, and Social Work. She divides her time between New York City's Greenwich Village and her home in the Catskill Mountains.